Word Bird™ Bird

Makes Words With Pig

Published in the United States of America by The Child's World®, Inc.
PO Box 326
Chanhassen, MN 55317-0326
800-599-READ
www.childsworld.com

Project Manager Mary Berendes
Editor Katherine Stevenson, Ph.D.
Designer Ian Butterworth

Library of Congress Cataloging-in-Publication Data
Moncure, Jane Belk.
Word Bird makes words with Pig : a short "i" adventure / by Jane Belk Moncure.
p. cm.
Summary: When his father brings home new word puzzles,
Word Bird makes up words with his friend Pig, and
each new word leads them into a new activity.
ISBN 1-56766-903-4 (lib. bdg.)
[1. Vocabulary. 2. Birds—Fiction. 3. Pigs—Fiction.] I. Title.
PZ7.M739 Wnp 2001
[E]—dc21
00-010894

Word Bird™

Makes Words With Pig

by Jane Belk Moncure

illustrated by Chris McEwan

"Did you bring some word puzzles?" asked Word Bird.

"I did," said Papa.

"I can make words in a jiffy," said Word Bird.

Word Bird put

p with ig.

What did Word Bird make?

p ig

Just then, Pig came to play.

"Hi, Pig."

"I can make words, too,"
said Pig.

Pig put

W with ig.

What word did Pig make?

wig

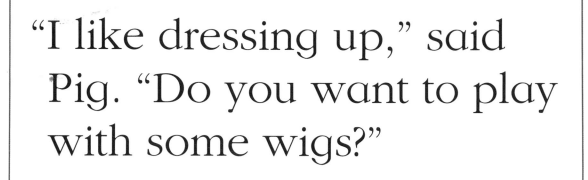

"I like dressing up," said Pig. "Do you want to play with some wigs?"

Pig put a wig on Word
Bird. "What a silly wig!"
Pig said.

Both Pig and Word Bird
giggled.

Then Pig put

What word did Pig make?

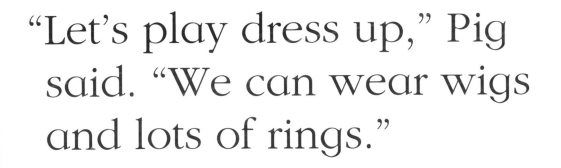

"Let's play dress up," Pig
said. "We can wear wigs
and lots of rings."

Word Bird put

k with ing.

What did Word Bird make?

k ing

They both played that they were kings until Pig began to sing.

Then Word Bird made
another word in a jiffy.
Word Bird put

sw with ing.

What did Word Bird make?

sw ing

"Let's go play on the swing," said Pig.

Word Bird gave Pig a big push on the swing.

Then Pig gave Word Bird a big push on the swing.

"I will make another word," said Pig.

Pig put

d with ish.

What word did Pig make?

d ish

"You need something in your dish," said Word Bird.

Just then, Mama said, "Come to dinner."

Pig filled the dish with figs.

After dinner, Pig helped
Word Bird wash the dishes.

"Now what can we do?"
asked Pig. Word Bird said,
"I will make another word,"
and put

sh with ip.

What did Word Bird make?

sh ip

"I have a ship," said Word Bird. "Let's take a trip in my ship."

So they did.

Pig said, "I know something else we can do."

Pig put

f with ish.

What word did Pig make?

f ish

"We can go fishing,"
Pig said.

They caught a
big, big fish…

but the fish slipped away!

Word bird said, "Let's get off this ship and go home in a jiffy."

"Let's race!" said Pig.
"I will win."

"No," said Word Bird.
"I will win."

Suddenly, Word Bird
tripped and slipped.

Pig said, "I win!"
Pig danced a silly
jig all the way home.

You can read more word
puzzles with Word Bird.

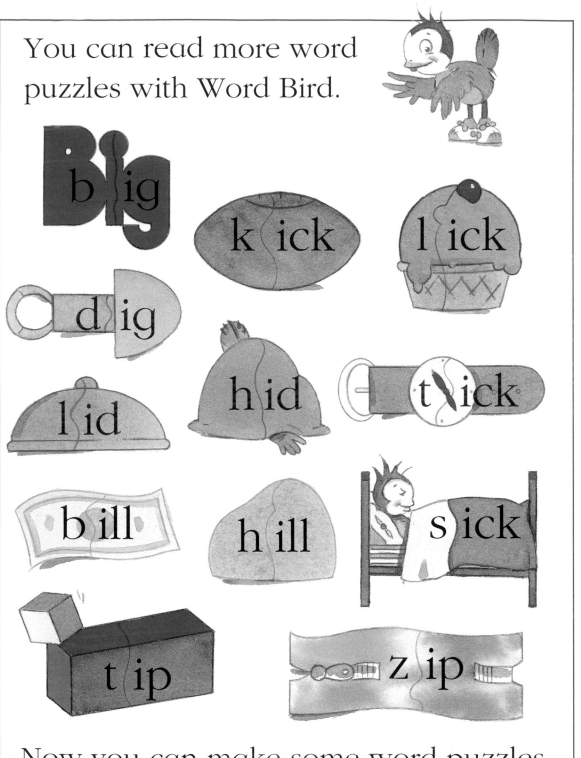

b ig

k ick

l ick

d ig

l id

h id

t ick

b ill

h ill

s ick

t ip

z ip

Now you can make some word puzzles.

34681

34681

McGRAW•HILL

HEALTH

SENIOR AUTHORS

Susan C. Giarratano-Russell

Donna Lloyd-Kolkin

PROGRAM AUTHORS

Danny J. Ballard

Alisa Evans Debnam

Anthony Sancho

 **McGraw-Hill**
School Division

New York   Farmington

PROGRAM AUTHORS

Susan C. Giarratano-Russell,
MSPH, Ed.D, CHES
Health Education Specialist
University Professor and Media Consultant
Glendale, California

Donna Lloyd-Kolkin, Ph.D.
Partner
Health & Education Communication
  Consultants
New Hope, Pennsylvania

Danny J. Ballard, Ed.D
Associate Professor, Health
Texas A & M University
College of Education
College Station, Texas

Alisa Evans Debnam, MPH
Health Education Supervisor
Cumberland County Schools
Fayetteville, North Carolina

Anthony Sancho, Ph.D.
Project Director
West Ed
Equity Center
Los Alamitos, California

PROGRAM REVIEWERS

Personal Health
Josey H. Templeton, Ed.D
Associate Professor
The Citadel, Military College of South Carolina
Charleston, South Carolina

Growth and Development
Jacqueline Ellis, M Ed, CHES
Health Education Consultant
Brunswick, Maine

Emotional and Intellectual Health
Donna Breitenstein, Ed.D
Professor of Health Education
Appalachian State University
Boone, North Carolina

Family and Social Health
Betty M. Hubbard, Ed.D, CHES
Professor, Department of Health Sciences
University of Central Arkansas
Conway, Arkansas

Nutrition
Celia J. Mir, Ed.D, RD, LD, CFCS
Associate Professor, Nutrition
University of Puerto Rico
Rio Piedras, Puerto Rico

Physical Fitness
James Robinson III, Ed.D
Visiting Professor of Health
Department of Health and Kinesiology
Texas A & M University
College Station, Texas

Disease Prevention and Control
Linda Stewart Campbell, MPH
Executive Director
Minority Task Force on AIDS
New York, New York

Alcohol, Tobacco, and Drugs
Kathleen Middleton, MS, CHES
Administrator for Health and Prevention
Monterey County Office of Education
Monterey County, California

Safety, Injury, and Violence Prevention
Philip R. Fine, Ph.D, MSPH
  Director
Wendy S. Horn, MPH
  Project Coordinator
Matthew D. Rousculp, MPH
  Assistant to the Director
Injury Control Research Center
University of Alabama at Birmingham
Birmingham, Alabama

Andrea D. Tomasek, MPH
Epidemiologist, Injury Prevention Division
Alabama Department of Public Health
Montgomery, Alabama

Community and Environmental Health
**Martin Ayong Ayim, Ph.D, MPH,
  BSPH, CHES**
Assistant Professor of Health Education
Grambling State University
Grambling, Louisiana

Teacher Reviewers
Miriam Kaeser, OSF
Assistant Superintendent
Archdiocese of Cincinnati
Cincinnati, Ohio

Christine Wilson
3rd Grade Classroom Teacher
Stout Field Elementary School
M.S.D. of Wayne Township
Indianapolis, Indiana

Multicultural Reviewer
Sylvia Pena, Ed.D
Dean, Graduate Studies
University of Texas at Brownsville
Brownsville, Texas

HEALTH ADVISORY BOARD MEMBERS

Lucinda Adams
State Advisor, Health Education
Former Director of Health
Dayton City Schools District
Dayton, Ohio

Clara Arch-Webster
Vice Principal
Duval County Schools
Jacksonville, Florida

Linda Carlton
Coordinator, Elementary Science & Health
Wichita, Kansas Public Schools USD 259
Wichita, Kansas

John Clayton
6th Grade Health Teacher
Orangewood Elementary School
Phoenix, Arizona

Pam Connolly
Subject Area Coordinator/HS Teacher
Diocese of Pittsburgh
Pittsburgh, Pennsylvania

Larry Herrold
Supervisor of Health Education, K–12
Baltimore County Public Schools
Baltimore, Maryland

Hollie Hinz
District Health Coordinator and
  Health Teacher
Menomonee Falls School District
Menomonee Falls, Wisconsin

Karen Mathews
5th Grade Teacher
Guilford County School
Greensboro, North Carolina

Patty O'Rourke
Health Coordinator
Cypress-Fairbanks I.S.D.
Houston, Texas

Sarah Roberts
6th Grade Health Teacher
McKinley Magnet School
Baton Rouge, Louisiana

Lindsay Shepheard
Health & Physical Education
  Program Coordinator
Virginia Beach City Public Schools
Virginia Beach, Virginia

Bob Wandberg
Health Education Curriculum & Instruction
Bloomington Public Schools
Bloomington, Minnesota

McGraw-Hill School Division

A Division of The McGraw-Hill Companies

Copyright © 2000 McGraw-Hill School Division, a Division of the Educational and
Professional Publishing Group of The McGraw-Hill Companies, Inc.

McGraw-Hill School Division
1221 Avenue of the Americas
New York, New York 10020

Printed in the United States of America
ISBN 0-02-277368-1 / 2
2 3 4 5 6 7 8 9 071 05 04 03 02 01 00 99

CONTENTS

CHAPTER **1**

GROWTH AND DEVELOPMENT 11

CHAPTER **2**

HANDBOOK

McGraw-Hill Health and the Health Pyramid

McGraw-Hill Health was created to help you be as healthy as you can be. The McGraw-Hill Health Pyramid shows what you need to reach the goal of good health.

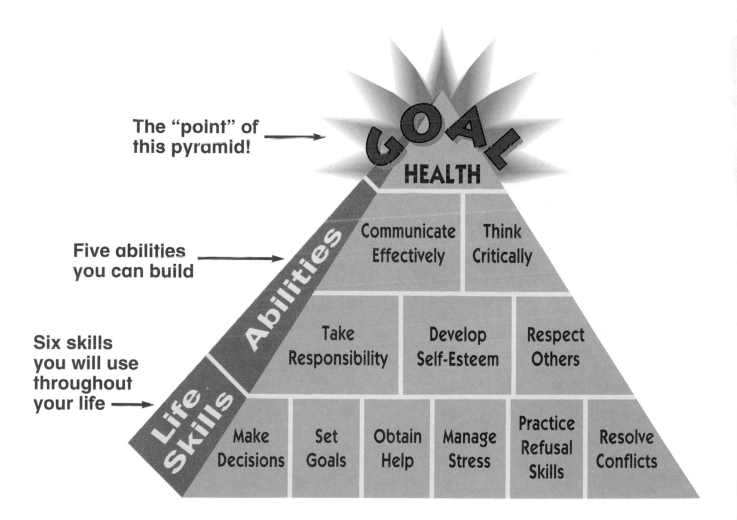

The "point" of this pyramid! →

GOAL

HEALTH

Five abilities you can build →

Abilities

Communicate Effectively

Think Critically

Take Responsibility

Develop Self-Esteem

Respect Others

Six skills you will use throughout your life →

Life Skills

Make Decisions

Set Goals

Obtain Help

Manage Stress

Practice Refusal Skills

Resolve Conflicts

PERSONAL HEALTH

You can do many things to keep yourself healthy.

CHAPTER CONTENTS

LESSON 1

What Is Good Health?

Good health means a healthy body. Good health means a healthy mind. It also means getting along with others.

Staying clean keeps you healthy. Being active keeps you healthy. Visit the doctor once a year for a checkup. The doctor also helps patients who are sick.

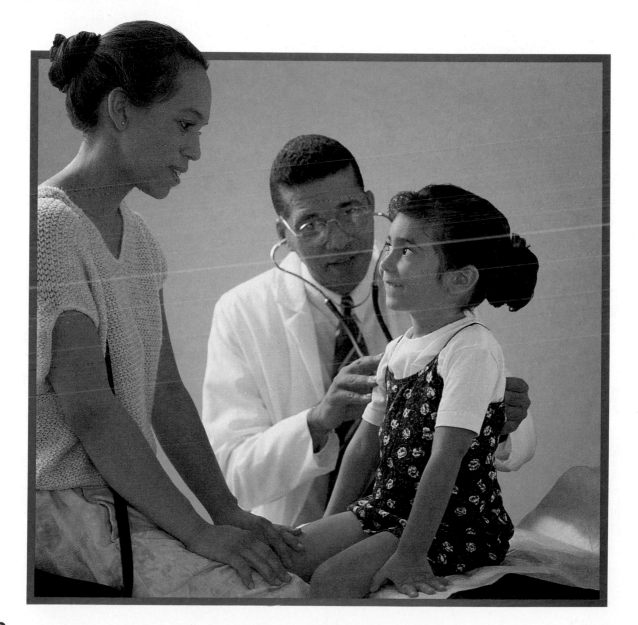

Good grooming means keeping your body clean. It also means taking care of the way you look.

Wash with soap and water. They clean your body. They wash off dirt and germs. Germs cause illness.

Always follow these three rules. Wash your hands before you eat. Wash them after playing. Wash them after using the toilet.

Good Grooming Products

LESSON 2

Rest and Sleep

Rest and sleep give your body energy. You need about 11 hours of sleep a night.

Getting too little rest and sleep can hurt your health. You may feel tired. You may feel grumpy with others. You may not do your best in school and at play.

Do the same things every night before going to sleep. Get to bed at the same time. Before bedtime, wash up and brush and floss your teeth.

Then do something quiet. You might enjoy a bedtime story. You might enjoy listening to soft music before going to sleep.

Most children have their 20 primary teeth by age three. Soon these first teeth fall out. By age six, permanent teeth grow in their place. Adults have 32 permanent teeth.

All teeth need good care. Eating healthful foods makes your teeth strong. Fruit, vegetables, and milk are good for your teeth. Sugary snacks can damage your teeth.

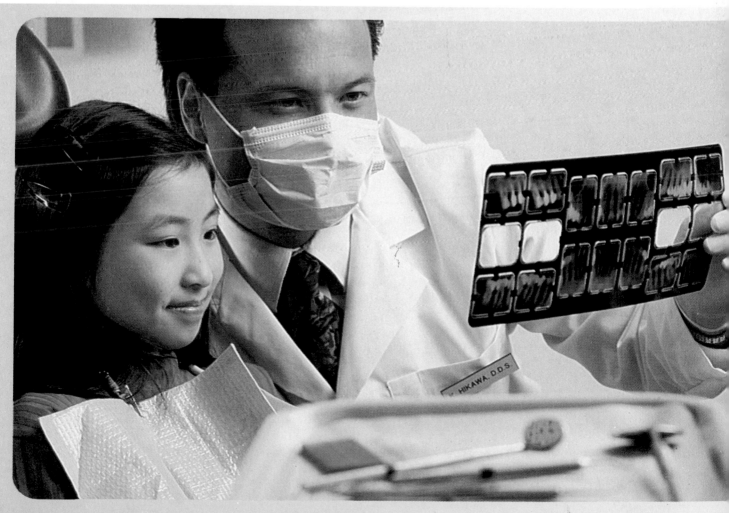

Visit a dentist for checkups two times each year. The dentist will look for cavities. The dentist also will clean your teeth.

Brush and floss every day to keep your teeth and gums healthy. Brushing gets rid of loose food and germs. Flossing cleans between teeth.

1. Brush the fronts of your teeth.

2. Brush the backs of your teeth.

3. Brush the tops of your teeth.

4. Floss between teeth.

LESSON 4

Taking Care of Eyes, Ears, and Skin

Your eyes, ears, and skin help you know what is happening around you. Your eyes help you see. Your ears help you hear. Your skin helps you feel things.

Hearing, seeing, and touching are senses. They keep you healthy and safe. They alert you to danger. That's why caring for them is important.

Your eyes and skin need to be protected from the sun. Sunglasses keep your eyes safe in bright light. Sunscreen protects your skin from sunburn.

Keep your ears safe from loud noises. Play music low and use earplugs, if needed. Always keep sharp objects away from your eyes, ears, and skin.

PROTECT YOUR SENSES

EYES

EARS

SKIN

A. Tell whether each sentence is **true** or **false**.

   1. You should wash your hands before eating.

   2. Only go to the doctor when you are sick.

   3. Good grooming habits keep you healthy.

B. Write **healthful** or **not healthful**.

C. Complete each sentence with a word from the box.

   6. _____ can damage your teeth.

   7. Use _____ to clean between your teeth.

floss   sweets

D. Which part of your body do these products protect?

8.   **9.**   **10.**

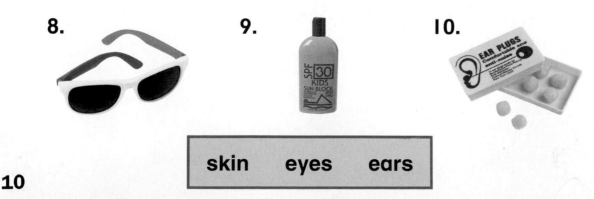

skin   eyes   ears

GROWTH AND DEVELOPMENT

Our bodies, minds, and feelings change and grow as we get older.

CHAPTER CONTENTS

LESSON 5 You Grow and Change

As you grow older, you change in many ways. Your body gets bigger. You grow taller and become heavier.

You can measure changes in your height with a yardstick. You can measure changes in your weight with a scale. How do you keep track of your growth?

All people grow and change. However, no two people grow and change in the same way.

As you grow older, you learn new skills. As a one year old, you just started to walk. Now, you can walk, jump, and run.

Growing older also means learning other new skills. Before you came to school, you already knew how to talk. At school, you began learning to read.

As you get older, you meet and make new friends. You learn to work and play with others.

Bones and muscles work together to help you move. The bones and muscles in your legs move as you walk. The bones and muscles in your arms move when you throw a ball.

Some of your bones also protect organs inside your body. For example, your skull bones protect your brain. Your brain helps you think. Your ribs are bones that protect your lungs. Your lungs help you breathe.

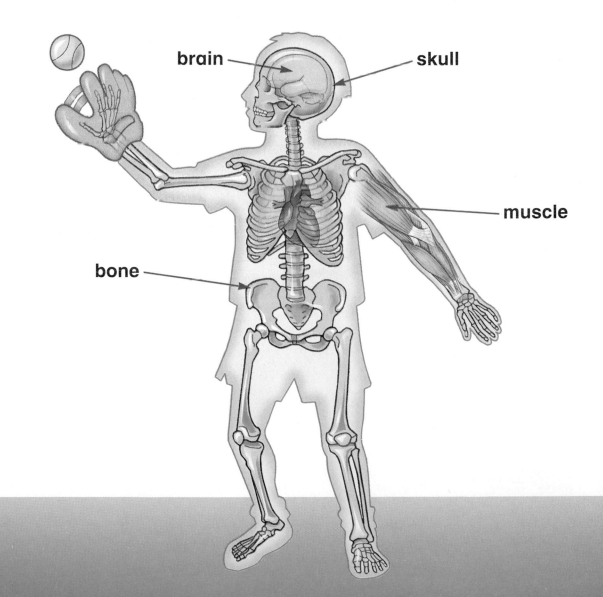

brain — skull

muscle

bone

Some muscles work without being attached to bones. Your heart is a muscle that works on its own. It never stops moving, even while you are asleep.

Like your brain and lungs, your heart is also an organ. It pumps blood throughout your body. Small tubes called blood vessels carry blood to all parts of the body.

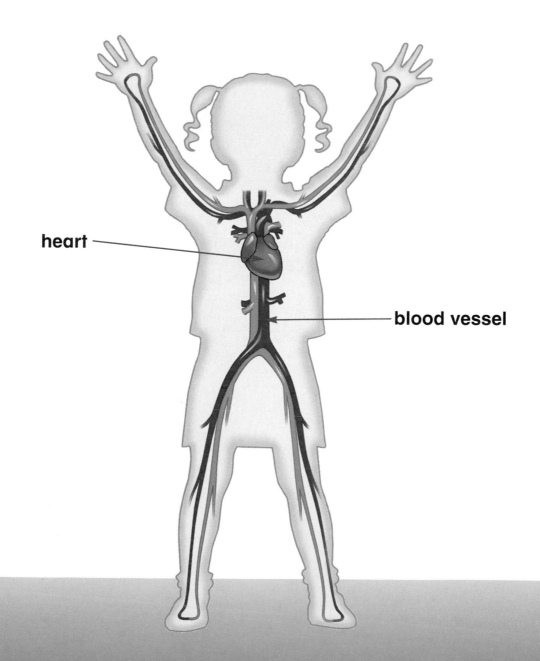

heart

blood vessel

LESSON 7 The Five Senses

Your five sense organs are your ears, eyes, skin, tongue, and nose. They tell you what is happening around you.

Your ears hear, your eyes see, and your skin can feel things. You smell with your nose and taste with your tongue. What senses are these children using?

You use your senses to get information from the outside world. The sense organs then send messages to the brain. When the messages arrive, your brain tells your body what to do.

For example, if there is a fire, you might see and smell smoke. You might hear a fire alarm. Your sense organs send this information to your brain. Your brain tells your body to move and get out of danger.

You change in many ways as you grow older, or age. The steps that people go through as they age are called the life cycle.

You started life as a baby and then became a child. Some day you will be a teenager. In time, you will become an adult and finally a senior citizen.

When you are an adult, your body is fully grown. However, your body will continue to change as you grow older. Your hair may become gray. Your skin may show some wrinkles.

You will continue to grow in other ways. You will keep on learning new things. You may try different jobs. You will go on making new decisions.

A. Write the word that names each body part.

bone
blood vessel
brain
muscle

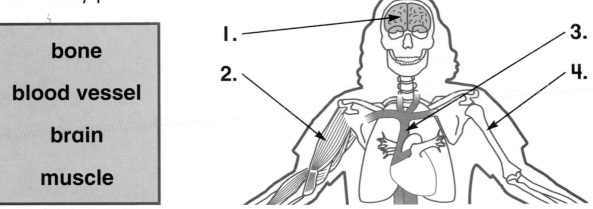

1.

2.

3.

4.

B. Write **true** or **false** for each statement.

5. Everyone grows in the same way.

6. As an adult your body is fully grown.

7. You stop learning new things when you become an adult.

8. Your five senses help you learn about the world around you.

C. What stage of the life cycle is shown in each picture?

9.

10.

EMOTIONAL AND INTELLECTUAL HEALTH

CHAPTER 3

THE BIG IDEA

Healthy people get along with others, feel good about themselves, and manage, or deal with, stress.

CHAPTER CONTENTS

LESSON 9

You and Your Feelings

Everyone has many different feelings. Feelings like happiness are nice. Other feelings, such as sadness, fear, and anger, are unpleasant.

Not everyone shows feelings in the same way. Some people become quiet when they are afraid. Other people get a stomachache.

Some people raise their voices or yell for help. Others may try to get away from what frightens them.

Happy feelings are easy to show. A smile, a laugh, a hug all can show happiness. It is also important to talk about feelings of sadness, anger, and fear.

Sometimes children and adults deal with these feelings in unhealthful ways. They may hit people or start a fight or say ugly things.

It is best if you share your feelings of sadness, anger, or fear. A trusted adult can help you learn healthful ways to deal with these feelings.

A friend is someone you care about and who cares about you. Friends enjoy playing and spending time together. They share their toys and games. They share ideas, stories, and jokes.

Friends also share their feelings. They are happy for each other when one of them does well. Friends try to help each other when one of them is sad or angry.

Our behavior, or actions, shows how we feel about our friends. Friends don't push each other or fight. They take turns. They don't say mean things to each other.

A friend does not want to harm you. Sometimes a friend may ask you to do something you know is wrong or dangerous. You can say "no" politely and firmly and still be friends.

Feeling Good About Yourself

All people have special talents, or things they do well. Maybe you are good at riding a bike or a skateboard. Your talent may be singing or drawing.

Our talents help us feel good about ourselves. When we like ourselves and what we do, we have self-esteem.

Everyone makes mistakes. Sometimes you may not do well at something you usually do easily. You also may make mistakes while learning new skills.

When something goes wrong, try to find out why. Then you can learn how to do better the next time. Feel good about the fact that you keep trying.

LESSON  12 Dealing with Stress

Have you ever gotten a stomachache before taking a test or speaking to the class? Many people feel nervous when they have to do something new or difficult.

These uncomfortable feelings are called stress. Stress may make your heart beat more quickly. Your breathing may become faster. Your mouth may become dry, or your hands may get sweaty.

Sometimes stress can be helpful. Feeling excited can make you do better. But most times, stress makes you feel uncomfortable.

You can learn ways to manage or deal with stress. You can take a walk or listen to quiet music.

Physical activity also helps you get rid of stress. Talking things over with a trusted adult or friend can help you feel better, too.

3 Show What You Know

A. Write **healthful** or **unhealthful** to tell how the child is showing feelings.

1.

2.

B. Write **true** or **false** for each sentence.

3. Everyone shows feelings in the same way.

4. Friends share happy times and sad times.

5. A good friend never says "no" to another friend.

6. Our actions show that we care about a friend.

7. All types of stress are bad for your health.

C. Write the word that completes each sentence.

8. A _____ is something that you do well.

9. Feeling good about yourself means you have _____.

10. The way your body reacts to something new or difficult is called _____.

self-esteem	talent	stress

FAMILY AND SOCIAL HEALTH

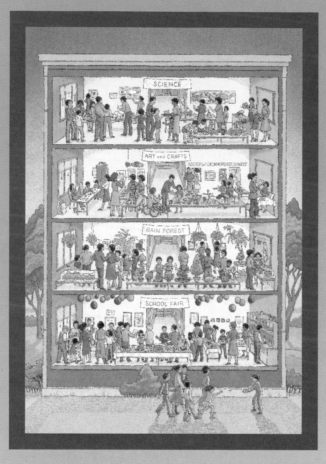

Getting Along with Your Family

The members of a family who live together make up a household. Members of a family respect each other. They are kind and honest. They love each other.

Family members try to help each other. They work together to get things done. Everyone has duties or responsibilities.

Parents give their children a home. They take care of all their children's needs. Children help their parents by doing household chores.

Every household needs rules to keep its members safe and to get things done. Making family rules is the job of parents. It is everyone's job to follow the rules.

Rules are meant to keep family members healthy. An important rule is eating healthful foods. Another household rule is putting away toys. This prevents people from tripping on them. Breaking rules can sometimes harm you.

Friends are people you know and like. Friends like to do things together. They share their thoughts and feelings.

Friends are honest and kind. They do not try to hurt your feelings. They do not ask you to do anything dangerous. You can count on them to help you when you need them. In what ways are these children being good friends?

What do you look for in a friend? A person's appearance, or looks, is only one part of a person. A person could have nice new clothes but be unkind.

The way a person thinks, acts, and speaks—his or her personality—is much more important. Friends are happy for you. They tell you that you did a good job. They say "thank you" when you help them. They say "I'm sorry" when they have upset you.

You and your classmates are in school to learn. A classroom has rules just like a healthy family. Everyone needs to work together to make the classroom a healthy place to learn.

Classmates must be honest and kind. They need to listen with respect to each other and to the teacher. They should offer help, or volunteer, whenever they can.

Everyone needs to follow rules for safety and order. Rules against running and pushing keep people from getting hurt. Rules about raising hands and taking turns keep the classroom in order.

The adults in charge of the school are the school staff. They are the principal, the teachers, the aides, the librarian, and the nurse. Their job is to help you learn and to keep you safe. Your job is to follow the rules and be helpful to others.

Show What You Know

A. Write the word that completes each sentence.

1. Breaking safety and health ＿＿ can cause injury or harm.

2. Washing dishes and taking out the garbage are examples of ＿＿.

3. Family members who live together make up the ＿＿.

| chores | household | rules |

B. Write **true** or **false** for each statement.

4. Friends never say "I'm sorry."

5. Friends never listen to each other.

6. Friends help each other whenever they can.

C. Which picture shows a school rule that keeps children safe? Which picture shows a school rule that keeps order in the classroom?

NUTRITION

A healthful diet contains a variety of balanced meals and healthful snacks.

CHAPTER CONTENTS

Food gives your body the energy to do things. Energy from food helps your body grow. It gives you the power to work and play.

Healthful foods keep your body healthy. They build strong bones and teeth. They also help your body fight illness.

Your body cannot use food as it is when you eat it. It must break down the food first. This is called digestion.

Digestion begins as your teeth grind food into little bits. It continues when the stomach churns food into liquid. Finally, food passes into the small intestine.

From there your body absorbs, or takes into the blood, what it needs from food. The part of food not needed passes through your body.

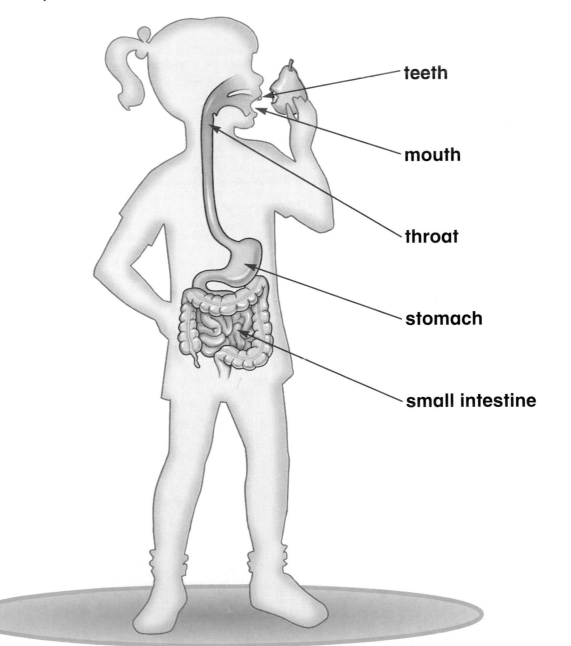

teeth

mouth

throat

stomach

small intestine

Some foods give the body lots of energy. Some foods help the body grow. Some make teeth and bones strong.

No one food does all these jobs well. That's why it's important to eat a variety of foods from different food groups.

Bread and Grain Group

Vegetable Group

Fruit Group

**Milk and Cheese
Group**

**Meat and Fish
Group**

Your body needs more food from some food groups and less food from others. The Food Guide Pyramid shows how much from each food group you should eat.

Each food group has a part of the Food Guide Pyramid. The bigger the part, the more servings you should eat every day. Should you eat more foods from the fruit group or from the bread and grain group?

FATS, OILS, AND SWEETS
Should be limited.

MEAT AND FISH GROUP
2–3 Servings

MILK AND CHEESE GROUP
2–3 Servings

FRUIT GROUP
2–4 Servings

VEGETABLE GROUP
3–5 Servings

BREAD AND GRAIN GROUP
6–11 Servings

At the very top of the Food Guide Pyramid are fats, oils, and sweets. These foods do not make up a food group.

The top is the smallest part of the Food Guide Pyramid. This means you should eat very little of the foods shown. Eating too many fats, oils, and sweets can hurt your teeth and heart. It may also cause you to gain a lot of weight.

EAT VERY LITTLE FOOD

WITH FATS

WITH OILS

WITH SUGAR

LESSON 18 — Balanced Meals

A meal is the food served and eaten at one time. Most people eat three meals—in the morning, at noon, and in the evening.

Each meal should be balanced. A balanced meal has foods from several food groups. The variety gives your body all the things it needs. A meal with only one or two food groups is not as healthful.

Balanced Breakfast

BALANCED MEALS

Balanced Lunch

Balanced Dinner

A serving is one portion of food. The Food Guide Pyramid tells how many servings of each food group you need every day.

The sizes of the servings are different for different food groups. One half cup of pasta, rice, or cereal is one serving from the bread and grain group. What would be one serving of cheese from the milk and cheese group?

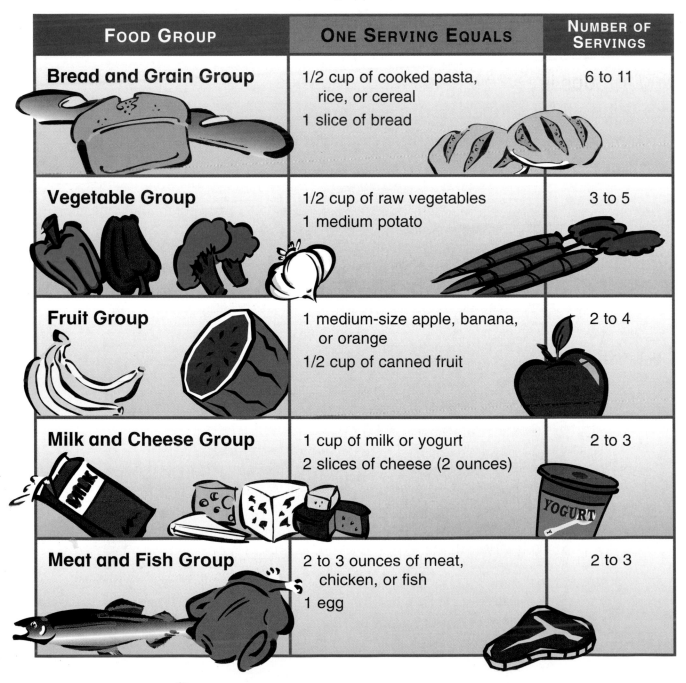

FOOD GROUP	ONE SERVING EQUALS	NUMBER OF SERVINGS
Bread and Grain Group	1/2 cup of cooked pasta, rice, or cereal 1 slice of bread	6 to 11
Vegetable Group	1/2 cup of raw vegetables 1 medium potato	3 to 5
Fruit Group	1 medium-size apple, banana, or orange 1/2 cup of canned fruit	2 to 4
Milk and Cheese Group	1 cup of milk or yogurt 2 slices of cheese (2 ounces)	2 to 3
Meat and Fish Group	2 to 3 ounces of meat, chicken, or fish 1 egg	2 to 3

Healthful Snacks

A snack is food that you eat between meals. Healthful snacks give your body extra energy. Snacks add to the variety of foods you eat. They help you balance your meals. Best of all, they can make a delicious break during a busy day.

Many snacks have too much salt, sugar, and fat. Salty pretzels, cupcakes, and fries are unhealthful snacks. Extra salt, sugar, and fat can lead to unhealthy weight gain and heart disease.

There are many tasty snack choices in the five food groups. Fruits are good snacks because they are naturally sweet. They give your body energy from natural sugar.

Avoid fatty snacks, but don't avoid all fat in your meals. Your body needs some fat to work well. Fat helps your body digest food. It also helps your muscles move well.

WHEN YOU WANT THIS SNACK

TRY THIS SNACK INSTEAD

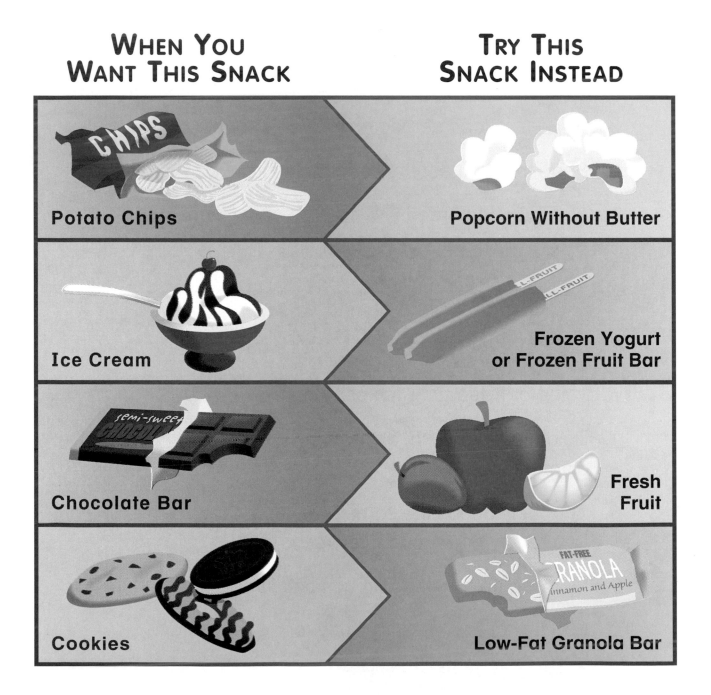

When You Want This Snack	Try This Snack Instead
Potato Chips	Popcorn Without Butter
Ice Cream	Frozen Yogurt or Frozen Fruit Bar
Chocolate Bar	Fresh Fruit
Cookies	Low-Fat Granola Bar

5 Show What You Know

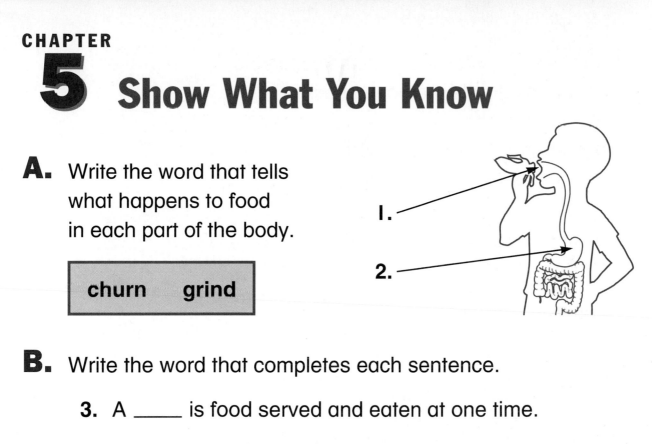

A. Write the word that tells what happens to food in each part of the body.

churn	grid

B. Write the word that completes each sentence.

3. A _____ is food served and eaten at one time.

4. Food that you eat between meals is a _____.

5. One portion of food is a _____.

6. Fruits are an example of a _____.

food group	meal	serving	snack

C. Write **true** or **false** for each sentence.

7. Balanced meals have food from several different food groups.

8. The body needs the same amount of food from each food group every day.

9. Many snacks have too much salt, sugar, or fat.

10. Foods that are too salty, fatty, or sweet are good for your health.

PHYSICAL ACTIVITY AND FITNESS

Physical activity makes you fit and healthy.

CHAPTER CONTENTS

LESSON 20 Physical Activity and the Body

Running and swimming make you breathe faster and your heart beat faster. These and other activities keep you fit. Physical fitness means that your body works well.

When you are fit, your muscles and heart are strong. You can bend and stretch easily. You can work and play hard without getting tired quickly. You keep your body at a healthy weight.

FITNESS MEANS

having a strong
heart and muscles

having a
healthy weight

not tiring
quickly

bending and
stretching easily

Your skeleton holds your body together.
It includes all the bones in your body. Many
bones have muscles attached to them.
Bones and muscles help you sit, stand,
and move.

Posture is the way you hold your body
upright. Strong muscles help you sit, stand,
and walk straight. Good posture improves
your health and helps you avoid injuries.

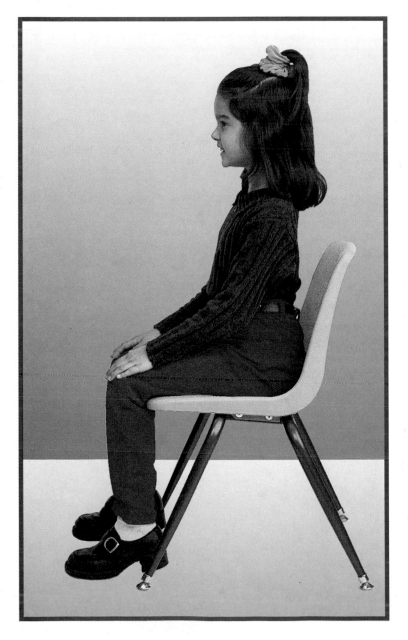

The President's Challenge

The President's Challenge is a physical fitness program with five exercises. If you take part in the program, you win an award.

Presidential Physical Fitness Award

National Physical Fitness Award

Participant Award

1 Curl-ups or Sit-ups

This exercise tells how strong your stomach muscles are.

2 Shuttle Run

This exercise tells how strong your leg muscles are. It also tells how long you can run without getting tired.

3 One Mile Run/Walk

This exercise tells how strong your leg muscles are. It also tells how strong your heart and lungs are.

4 Pull-ups

This exercise tells how strong your arm and shoulder muscles are.

5 V-sit Reach

This exercise tells how easily you can bend and stretch your legs and back.

LESSON 21
Developing a Fitness Plan

Physical activities keep you fit. They make your heart, lungs, and muscles strong. They help you bend and stretch. They also help you work hard without getting tired quickly.

You can build other skills to become more fit. You can improve your balance, staying upright without falling.

You can learn to use several parts of your body at once. You can also learn to move quickly and easily.

Exercise is physical activity. It builds fitness skills. Jumping rope is an exercise. Always warm up before you exercise. Moving slowly and stretching make your heart beat faster. They get your muscles ready to work.

Your exercises should start slowly and then get harder and faster. After you exercise, do slower activities to get your body to cool down.

1. Warm Up

2. Exercise

3. Cool Down

6 Show What You Know

A. Write **good posture** or **poor posture**.

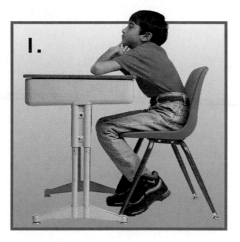

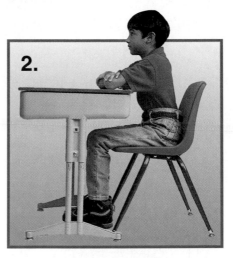

B. Write the word that completes each sentence.

3. Bending and stretching easily are _____ skills.

4. Running makes your _____ stronger.

5. Physical activity that builds fitness skills is _____.

| exercise | fitness | heart |

C. Tell if each sentence is **true** or **false**.

6. Warm ups are an important part of exercise.

7. Exercising will not improve your balance.

8. Stretching is a good warm-up activity.

DISEASE PREVENTION AND CONTROL

CHAPTER
7

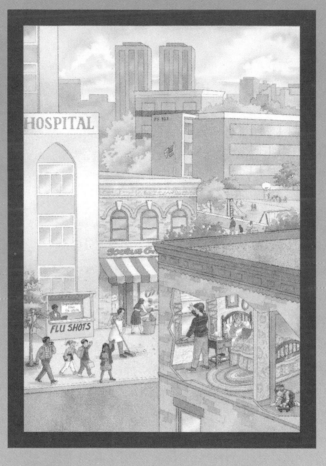

Germs are very tiny living things. They are so tiny that you can't even see them. Germs cause colds and the flu. They also cause mumps, measles, chicken pox, and other illnesses.

Your body tells you when you are getting sick. You may have a sore throat or runny nose. You may cough or sneeze. Your body may feel very warm from a fever.

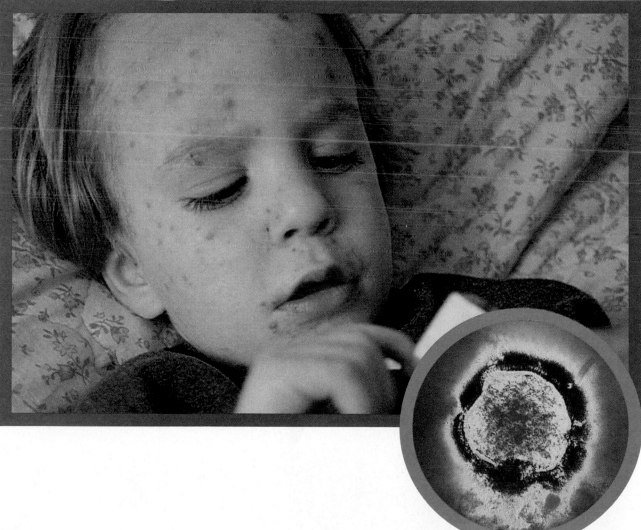

Coughs and sneezes spread germs through the air. Germs spread when you touch someone who has a cold or flu. Using an unwashed glass or sharing food is another way germs are spread.

Germs get into the body through the mouth, eyes, ears, and nose. They also may enter the body through cuts, scrapes, and insect and animal bites.

WAYS GERMS ENTER THE BODY

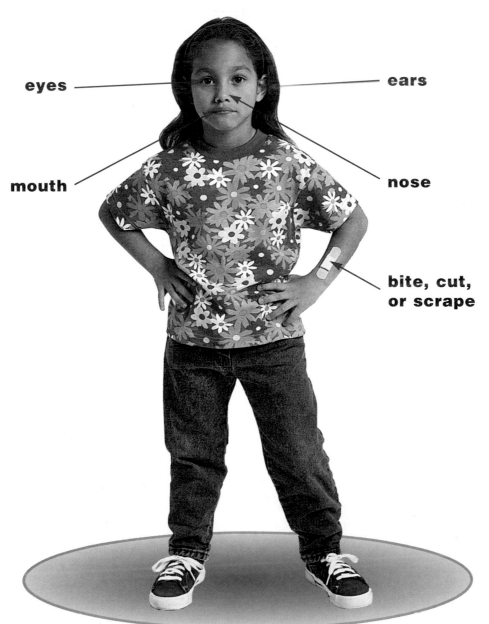

eyes

ears

mouth

nose

bite, cut, or scrape

You can stay healthy by stopping germs from entering your body. Washing your hands with soap and warm water kills many germs on them. Always wash your hands before eating and after using the bathroom. Be sure to clean and cover cuts or scrapes.

Don't share food or drinks with a sick person. If you are sick, you can prevent your germs from spreading. Always cover your mouth and nose when you cough or sneeze.

Wash Hands

Cover Nose and Mouth

WAYS TO STOP GERMS

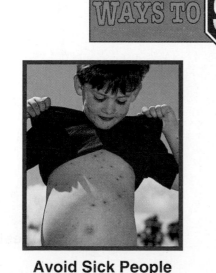

Avoid Sick People

Clean and Cover Cuts

Many illnesses caused by germs are easily spread. Almost everyone gets a cold or flu. However, some illnesses are not caused by germs and cannot be spread. These are illnesses such as asthma.

A strong body will help you avoid illness. It also will help you recover, or get better quickly, when you do get sick. Keep your body strong by eating healthful foods. Also get plenty of exercise and lots of rest.

Be Physically Active

WAYS TO KEEP YOUR BODY STRONG

Eat Healthful Foods

Get Sleep and Rest

When you feel sick, tell your parent or a trusted adult. You may need to see a doctor. The doctor may give you medicine to help you get better.

Medicines cure an illness you already have. Some medicines are pills or liquids that you swallow. Other medicines are given as shots. The doctor puts the medicine into your body with a needle.

MEDICINES COME IN MANY FORMS

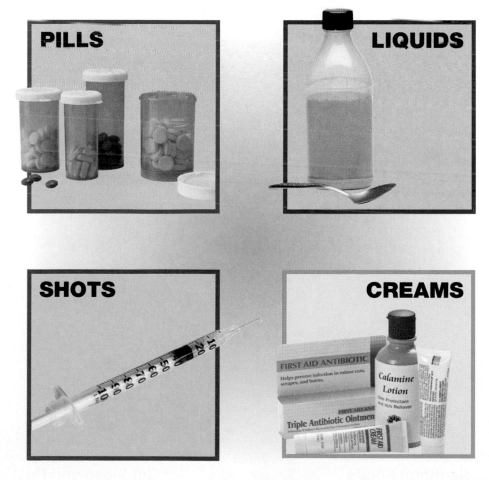

PILLS

LIQUIDS

SHOTS

CREAMS

You may visit the doctor for a checkup to stay healthy. The doctor may give you a vaccine. Vaccines are medicines that keep you from getting sick. They help your body fight germs that cause certain illnesses. Vaccines can prevent illnesses such as the measles.

Some vaccines can be taken by mouth. Many vaccines are given as shots. Vaccines have stopped the spread of some very dangerous illnesses.

A. Write a sentence about the health rule shown in each picture.

B. Write **true** or **false** for each sentence.

3. Germs can be spread by drinking from the same glass as a sick person.

4. Germs can be spread by sneezing or coughing into the air.

5. All illnesses are caused by germs.

6. Eating healthful foods helps your body fight germs.

7. Getting enough sleep and rest keeps your body strong.

C. Write the word that completes each sentence.

8. When you are sick, the doctor may give you _____ to help you get better.

9. Measles can be prevented by a _____.

10. Medicines you take by swallowing are _____.

| pills | medicine | vaccine |

ALCOHOL, TOBACCO, AND DRUGS

THE BIG IDEA

Medicines can help keep you healthy. Alcohol, tobacco, and illegal drugs damage your health.

CHAPTER CONTENTS

A drug is something you take that makes changes in the body. Medicines are drugs that can improve a person's health.

Some medicines help a person get better. Other medicines can stop a person from getting sick.

Never take a medicine on your own or from a friend. Only take medicine from a trusted adult. Medicine should always be stored safely away from children.

Most medicines are safe when used correctly. It is legal to buy many medicines in stores. Some medicines can only be bought and used with a doctor's order, or prescription.

Other drugs, like marijuana, are illegal. It is against the law to buy, sell, or use them. Illegal drugs are dangerous. They are never good for your health. They can never be used safely.

LESSON 26 Tobacco and Health

Tobacco is a plant. Its leaves are dried to make cigarettes, cigars, and pipe tobacco for people to smoke. Chewing tobacco is also made from tobacco leaves.

Tobacco contains a harmful drug called nicotine. People who use tobacco for a while develop a strong need for nicotine. Then it becomes very hard to stop using tobacco.

Using tobacco is always harmful to a person's health. Tobacco products may damage a person's lungs and cause heart disease. Cancer may develop in the lungs, mouth, throat, or stomach of a tobacco user.

Say "no" to anyone who offers you tobacco. Tell them that it is not good for your health. Tell them your parents will not allow it. Tell them it is against the law to offer tobacco to anyone 18 and under. Walk away from the person if you must.

THE EFFECTS OF TOBACCO ON THE BODY

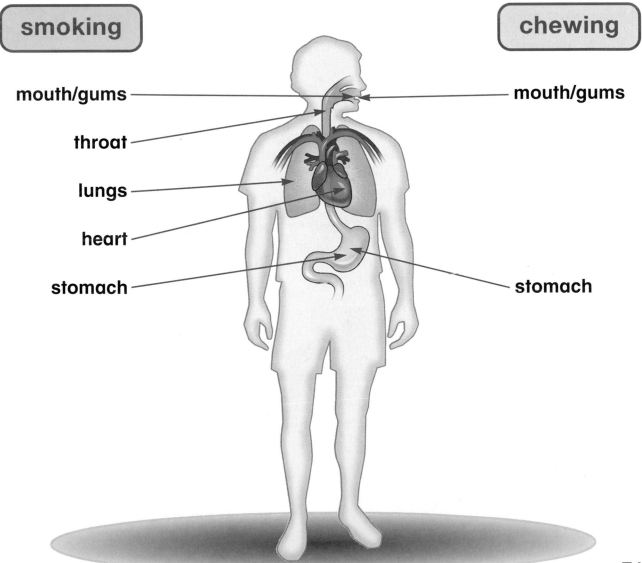

smoking

chewing

mouth/gums

throat

lungs

heart

stomach

mouth/gums

stomach

Alcohol is a drug found in beer, wine, and liquor. It is also found in some medicines. Alcohol changes the way the body works. These changes happen soon after a person drinks it.

Alcohol may cause a drinker to become dizzy and lose balance. Drinkers often think unclearly or slur words. Drivers who drink alcohol may get into accidents. They may react too slowly to prevent accidents and injuries.

People who drink alcohol often can develop a strong need for it. This need is called addiction. This need can make it hard for them to stop. After many years, alcohol can damage the brain, heart, liver, and stomach.

Say "no" to someone who offers you alcohol. Say that alcohol is unhealthy. Explain that it is against the law for you to drink. Remember that you can walk away.

THE EFFECTS OF ALCOHOL ON THE BODY

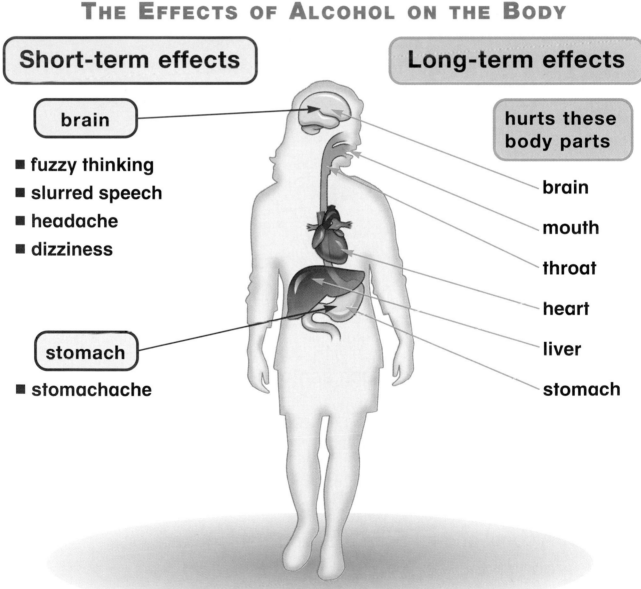

Short-term effects

brain
- fuzzy thinking
- slurred speech
- headache
- dizziness

stomach
- stomachache

Long-term effects

hurts these body parts

brain

mouth

throat

heart

liver

stomach

A. Complete each sentence with the correct word.

1. A drug that can improve a person's health is called a ____.

2. Some medicines can only be bought with a doctor's ____.

3. Only take medicine from a doctor, nurse, parent, or other trusted ____.

| adult | medicine | prescription |

B. Write **tobacco**, **alcohol**, or **both** to tell which harms each body part.

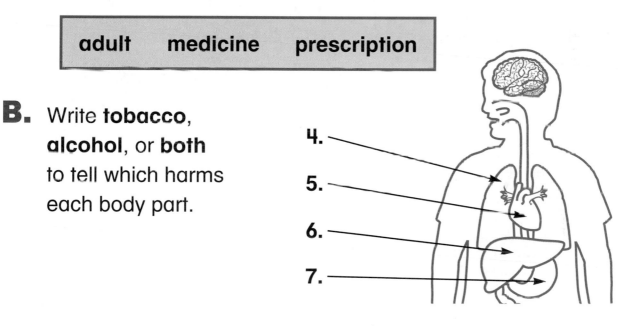

4.

5.

6.

7.

C. Write **true** or **false** for each sentence.

8. Tobacco products can cause cancer and heart disease.

9. All drugs are medicines.

10. Alcohol and tobacco products can cause addiction.

SAFETY AND INJURY PREVENTION

THE BIG IDEA

Most injuries can be prevented by following safety rules, avoiding hazards, and asking for help when you need it.

CHAPTER CONTENTS

Many household products are hazards. Some products used for cleaning, painting, or gluing can cause harm. They are not safe to eat, drink, touch, or inhale. The chemicals in them can make a person sick or even kill a person.

Always look at product labels and warnings. The picture of a skull and crossbones means there is poison in a product. Some labels have other warning signs.

Only adults should use household products. They should be stored where children cannot reach them. Never use household products on your own. Never let them come in contact with your skin or eyes.

Never inhale or breathe in fumes or odors from household products. These products should only be used in a room with open windows.

LESSON 29 — Safety Outdoors

Always cross the street at the crosswalk or intersection. Obey the traffic light. Cross only when the light is green.

Be sure to look both ways before you cross. Look left, right, and then left again. Watch for cars and bicycles turning corners. Obey the crossing guard if there is one.

Always use a safety belt when you ride in a car. If possible, use a safety belt in a bus. Sit quietly and don't get out of your seat. Never bother the driver.

When you ride a bike, always ride on the right side of the road. Be sure to wear a safety helmet. Always steer with both hands. Watch for cars leaving the curb.

Keep a single line if you are biking with friends. Always ride one person to a bicycle. Learn the hand signals for a right turn, a left turn, and a stop. Walk—don't ride—your bike across an intersection.

STOP

CAUTION

GO

RIGHT TURN   **LEFT TURN**   **STOP**

Always get away from a fire if you see one. Flames, smoke, sparks, and heat make a fire very dangerous. If you see a fire or fire hazard, tell an adult right away.

Matches, worn wires, and overloaded electric sockets are fire hazards. Some liquids, such as oil and kerosene, are also hazards. Never play with a fire hazard. If your clothes catch fire, always "Stop, drop, and roll" to put the fire out.

1. STOP

2. DROP

3. ROLL

A fire drill helps you practice being safe in case of a real fire. Learn where fire exits are at school. Always follow safety rules during a fire drill.

FIRE DRILL RULES

1. Don't talk.
2. Line up.
3. Listen to your teacher.
4. Follow directions.
5. Get to the exit quickly.

When you are home alone, stay away from hazards. Avoid dangerous household products. Never touch a gun or point it at anyone. Avoid scissors, knives, or other sharp objects.

Stay away from hot things like toasters or irons. Be careful not to trip on clutter. Pick up piles of paper and toys left on the floor.

Don't behave in a way that creates indoor hazards. Running, pushing, or throwing things can cause injuries.

Always lock the door when you are home alone. If a stranger comes to the door, don't open it. Never say you are alone. If the stranger won't leave, call the police or a trusted adult.

Never tell a stranger who calls on the phone that you are home alone. Tell the stranger your parent is too busy to take the call. Offer to take a message.

EMERGENCY NUMBERS

POLICE AND FIRE	911
MOM AT WORK	999-1101
DAD AT WORK	511-8822
GRANDMA	444-4133
AUNT JANE	444-2167
MRS. BRIGHT	444-6543

LESSON 32 Good Touch/ Bad Touch

Everyone wants to be treated in a kind and friendly way. Someone who shows you respect treats you the way you want to be treated.

Hugs and kisses between family members are signs of caring. They are good touches. So are pats on the back and handshakes between friends.

Sometimes, people may treat you in a mean, unfriendly, or scary way. This behavior shows disrespect. Shoves, slaps, and punches are bad touches. Bad touches are never signs of caring.

Always say "no" to bad touches. Tell a trusted adult right away if someone gives you a bad touch and tells you to keep it a secret.

LESSON 33 — First Aid

A scrape on your knee or a cut on your finger is a minor injury. It isn't serious, but you should take care of the injury right away. The immediate care for an injury or sickness is called first aid.

Some injuries and illnesses are very serious. They are emergencies. They need immediate care from an adult or health-care worker.

RULES FOR AN EMERGENCY

- Tell an adult right away.
- If no adult is near, call 911 or 0 for help.
- Tell the operator your name.
- Tell the operator what the emergency is.
- Tell where the emergency is.

A. What does each picture mean?

 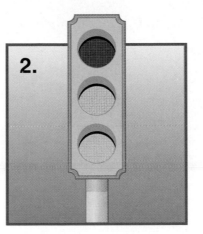

B. Write **true** or **false** for each sentence.

3. If your clothes catch fire, have a friend put it out.

4. Never inhale fumes from household products.

5. Always wear a safety helmet when bike riding.

6. It's okay to open your door to a stranger.

7. If you see an emergency, tell an adult or call 911.

C. Write the word that completes each sentence.

8. Paint, glue, and cleaning products are _____ hazards.

9. Matches and worn wires are _____ hazards.

10. Papers and toys on the floor are examples of _____.

| clutter | fire | household |

COMMUNITY AND ENVIRONMENTAL HEALTH 10

THE BIG IDEA

Members of a community share the responsibility of promoting health and caring for the environment.

CHAPTER CONTENTS

LESSON 34

Community Health Workers

Health-care workers help people in the community stay healthy and safe. Doctors, nurses, dentists, and pharmacists are health-care workers.

EMS workers also provide health care. EMS workers travel in ambulances. They give help to people in emergencies.

Some health-care workers do their jobs in hospitals or clinics. Others go to the homes of the sick and elderly.

People go to a hospital for many reasons. They may be sick. They may be having a baby, or they may need a health test.

Most hospitals have an emergency room. A person who is injured or very ill can go there for immediate help.

A clinic is a place in the community where people can get health care. Some clinics help people with their teeth or with other health needs.

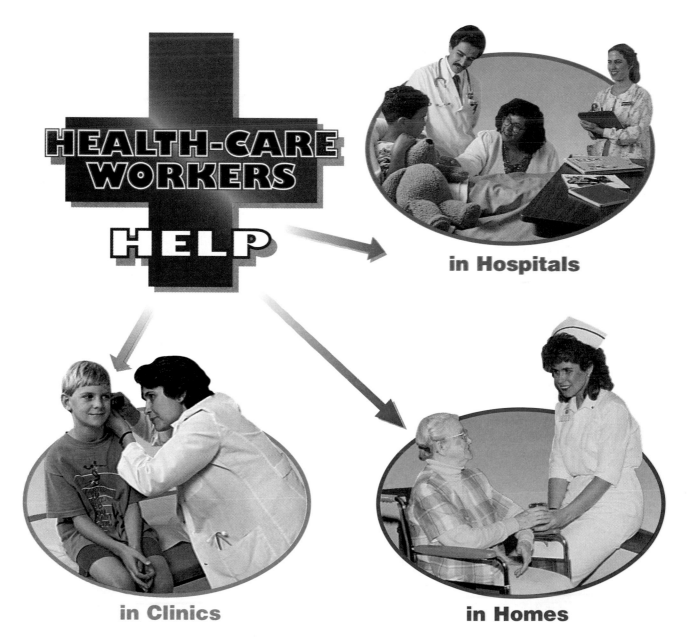

HEALTH-CARE WORKERS HELP

in Hospitals

in Clinics

in Homes

LESSON 35 Pollution's Effect on Health

Your environment includes everything around you. Pollution means that part of the environment is unclean. Pollution is harmful to the health of people, animals, and plants in the community.

Air pollution can harm lungs. Water pollution can poison drinking water. Land pollution can bring disease-causing animals.

AIR

WATER

LAND

Communities have laws to control pollution. Everyone can help to keep the environment clean.

Follow community rules. Recycle glass, plastic, paper, and metal products. Reuse things rather than throw them away. Reduce how much water, paper, and other products you use.

STOP POLLUTION

RECYCLE   **REDUCE**   **REUSE**

RECYCLE
WHITE PAPER ONLY

LESSON 36

Keeping the Environment Clean

A clean neighborhood helps to keep the people who live there healthy. Sanitation workers keep a neighborhood clean by picking up the garbage.

Garbage can damage the health of people in the community. Garbage will pollute the air with bad smells. It may also attract insects and disease-causing animals.

Everyone must work to keep the neighborhood clean. Be sure to throw litter into trash baskets. Follow community rules for getting rid of garbage.

Reduce the amount of water that you use. Save water by not letting it run while brushing teeth or washing dishes.

A. Complete each sentence with the correct word.

1. Doctors, nurses, and dentists are _____ workers.

2. Most hospitals have _____ rooms where people who need immediate help can go.

3. A neighborhood place where people can get health care is a _____.

clinic	emergency	health-care

B. Name the type of pollution shown in each picture.

4.

5.

C. Write **true** or **false** for each sentence.

6. Sanitation workers keep neighborhoods clean by putting litter in garbage cans.

7. Pollution is harmful to the health of people, animals, and plants in the community.

8. Reusing products helps to control pollution.

Life Skill 1: Make Decisions

Part of growing up is making your own decisions. Some decisions only matter for today. What to wear to school matters only for the day.

Some decisions are important for a long time. Eating healthful foods is a life-long decision.

Here's how you can make decisions.

Life Skill 1

MAKE DECISIONS

1. See that you need to make a decision.

2. State the problem.

3. List some choices you could make.

4. Think about how each choice could come out.

5. Decide on one of the choices.

6. Make sure you made a good decision.

Life Skill 2: Set Goals

A goal is something you want to do. It is something you must work for. You might set a goal to be a good soccer player.

Here's how you can set goals.

Life Skill 2

SET GOALS

1. Choose a goal. Write it down.

2. List things needed to reach the goal.

3. List people who can help you reach the goal.

4. Set a time to reach the goal.

5. Check how you are doing.

6. When you reach the goal, reward yourself.

98

Life Skill 3: Obtain Help

Part of good health is knowing when you need help. You can get help from many different people. A trusted adult can help with many problems. Police or firefighters can be called in an emergency.

Here's how you can obtain help.

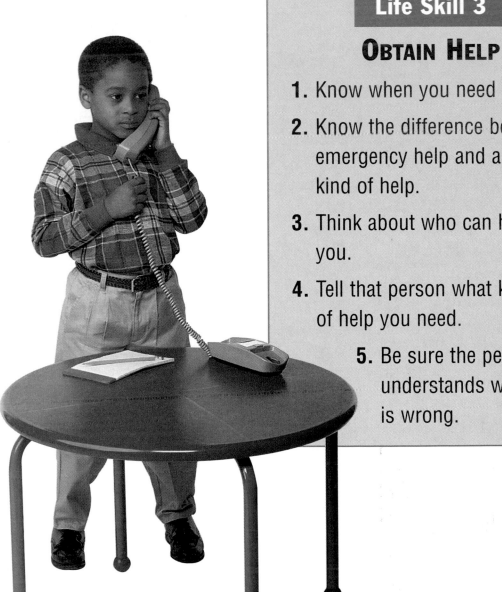

Life Skill 3

OBTAIN HELP

1. Know when you need help.

2. Know the difference between emergency help and another kind of help.

3. Think about who can help you.

4. Tell that person what kind of help you need.

5. Be sure the person understands what is wrong.

Life Skill 4: Manage Stress

Stress is an uncomfortable feeling. It can be caused by people, places, or things. Sometimes stress can be helpful. Too much stress is not good. You might have trouble sleeping, eating, or doing your homework.

Here's how you can manage stress.

Life Skill 4

MANAGE STRESS

1. Plan how you spend your time.

2. Gets lots of rest, sleep, and physical activity.

3. Eat healthful foods.

4. Try to relax. Take deep breaths.

5. Talk with a trusted friend or adult.

Life Skill 5: Practice Refusal Skills

One way to stay healthy is to say "no." Refusal skills help you say "no" to something that is wrong or not healthful.

To decide when to say "no," think about what is right for you. Ask yourself, "Is this good for me?"

Here's how you can practice refusal skills.

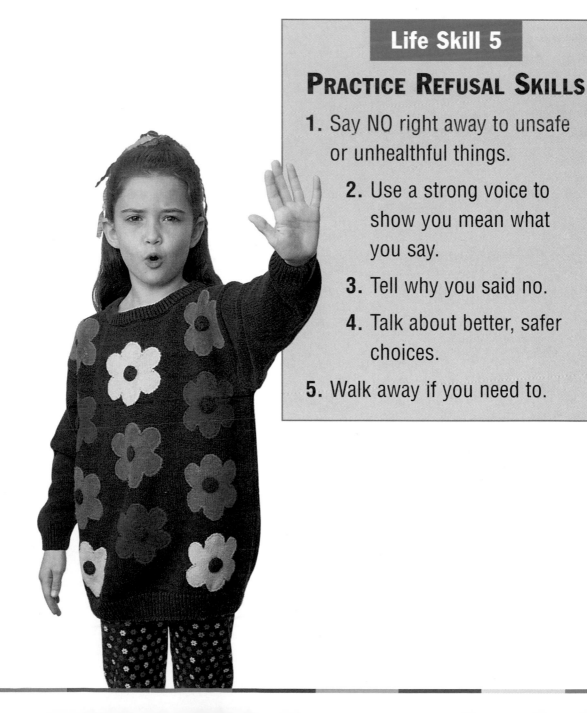

Life Skill 5

PRACTICE REFUSAL SKILLS

1. Say NO right away to unsafe or unhealthful things.

2. Use a strong voice to show you mean what you say.

3. Tell why you said no.

4. Talk about better, safer choices.

5. Walk away if you need to.

Life Skill 6: Resolve Conflicts

People do not always have the same likes and dislikes. Sometimes they disagree. A strong disagreement is a conflict.

Stay away from a conflict when you can. If you can't, find a way to end it peacefully.

Here are five steps you can follow to resolve conflicts.

Life Skill 6

RESOLVE CONFLICTS

1. Accept people as they are.

2. Don't call people names. Don't make fun of them.

3. Try to understand how the other person feels.

4. Try to meet the other person halfway without doing anything unhealthful or unsafe.

5. Think about talking it over later. If you must, just walk away.

CREDITS